INFINITE HAPPINESS

FINDING YOUR WAY THROUGH
THE ART OF SELF-REFLECTION

HEIDI CARLIN, RYT

BALBOA.
PRESS

A DIVISION OF HAY HOUSE

Balboa Press books may be ordered through booksellers or by contacting:

Balboa Press
A Division of Hay House
1663 Liberty Drive
Bloomington, IN 47403
www.balboapress.com
1 (877) 407-4847

Print information available on the last page.

ISBN: 978-1-5043-8429-2 (sc)
ISBN: 978-1-5043-8430-8 (hc)
ISBN: 978-1-5043-8431-5 (e)

Library of Congress Control Number: 2017911174

Balboa Press rev. date: 08/08/2017

CONTENTS

INTRODUCTION – HOW TO USE THIS JOURNAL

M y intention for this self-help journal is to share my story of living with depression and anxiety and supporting you in your journey to wellness. I provide you with thought-provoking journaling opportunities to show you it is possible to live a wholesome life, even when challenges arise.

This journal includes inspirational messages, discussion on why these messages are relevant, and space after each to allow you to express your thoughts by journaling on what comes to mind. You are welcome to skip around, maybe even open the book randomly, and work on the message that appears between your fingers that day. I encourage you to work with each message as long as you like. Some of you may want to work with one inspirational message a day, or look at a new message once a week, or once a month. Whatever frequency resonates with you, please use your intuition.

I intend for these messages to give you strength and courage to bring out the best you already are inside. Some messages may not resonate with you at all, and that is perfectly okay. My wish for you is to know that you are never alone, you have support in this World, and this Universe always has your back, no matter how dark your days may seem. I hope you come to realize after working with this journal that everything happens for a reason, and the highest good will always come from each event, no matter how bad it may seem in the moment.

The grand scheme of the Universe is always in support of you, no matter what.

This journal is broken into five major sections that discuss these overall themes:

1. Meditation – Hearing your Inner Voice
2. Naikan – The Art of Gratitude
3. Reiki – The Universal Energy of Love
4. Spirituality – What it means to You
5. Healing Tools – Continue finding Happiness

Each themed section has five inspirational messages each you can work with.

If you would like to connect with me further, or work with me, please contact me at www.reikiwithheidi.com. You will find additional resources on this website and how to contact me. Please "Like" my Facebook page at www.facebook.com/reikiwithheidi where I post weekly Oracle Card readings and other helpful information to guide you along your journey to happiness.

A little bit about me. I have been married for over 20 years to a man who supports me through thick and thin, have a cat named Samuel, and I love hiking and reading books. I am a Registered Yoga Teacher, Shaman, Reiki Master, Essential Oil Enthusiast, and a Gemini. I have also been struggling with depression and anxiety for many years. Throughout my journey to coping with depression and anxiety, I have picked up tools, techniques, and ways of moving on, even when it feels unbearable to get out of bed some mornings. I want to share these tools with you so you know it is possible to feel better, even when all seems hopeless (and trust me, I've been there more than once).

Please note that some tools may be excellent for you, and some may not. Part of this Journal, indeed, this Journey called Life, is to find out what resonates with you, and what does not. I am here for you, should you find the need to talk, and I look forward to connecting with you. Enjoy your Journey!

I. MEDITATION –
HEARING YOUR INNER VOICE

In my humble opinion, pretty much anything can be called meditation. Sitting cross legged and practicing emptying the mind is probably the most traditional way of thinking about meditation. But I have come to realize there are many ways to meditate. Taking a walk in the woods or on the beach, anywhere in nature, really, can be a form of meditation. Writing in your journal about what comes to mind is a form of meditation. Drawing or painting is a way to meditate.

The main point of meditation is really just to empty the mind of mundane or scattered thoughts and to contemplate the present; focusing on what is immediately in front of you at that moment. Many westerners are intimidated by practicing meditation, but I believe everyone can do it, especially since I can do it. And trust me, I am scatter brained and very easily distracted. In writing this paragraph alone, I had several non-related thoughts arise, and I was able to pull myself back to this page.

The trick with meditation is to practice non-judgment. Okay, I sat down to meditate, and my grocery list came into my head instead. Fine. Now let's get back to emptying my mind and moving past the grocery list; I wonder what else there is that will come up!

Simply accepting and acknowledging when you are getting side tracked, and not judging yourself for it is, I believe, a main concept of practicing effective meditation, no matter what form of meditation you choose.

Let us practice meditation together. Let me show you how it has helped in my life, and show you there is no right or wrong way, just your way, to practicing becoming the more mindful person you may want to be. Explore the different ways to meditate and see what resonates. Enjoy!

Meditation Message 1: Breathe deeply. It really does bring calmness.

Why: I am a Registered Yoga Teacher and we have always been taught to breathe deeply when you are in Yoga class. When doing Viniyoga, my favorite kind of therapeutic Yoga, we often match our movement with our breath. It has an amazingly calming and focusing effect on me. Staying present has often been a challenge for me, especially when I am feeling particularly anxious that day. It's so easy to start thinking about things that worry you, and then you realize that worry is totally irrational, and then you think about how silly you are being so irrational, but then your anxious mind tells you, no it's real, you really should worry about this…. and it goes on and on. Have you been there? Yeah, me too.

When I go down that highway of scary thoughts, I try my best to tap the brakes and take the Deep Breath exit. When I begin to take that first deep breath, my mind instantly takes a tiny break. I can feel my mind re-center. Ah, that feels better. But often, by the second breath, I'm back to worrying. Okay, that's fine. Just keep breathing. And so I do. And then I start to count: breathe in for 1, 2, 3, 4, breathe out for 1, 2, 3, 4. Repeat at least four times. I promise you will feel a tiny difference. And you might want to do it again next time you're feeling overwhelmed.

Your turn: Write a sentence about how you feel right now. Then sit quietly and breathe counting to 4 on the inhale and to 4 on the exhale four times. Next, practice the same breath while moving your arms above your head while inhaling and moving them back down to your side while exhaling four times. Close your eyes to really focus on the breath and movement. Write about how you feel now. Has anything shifted? Do you notice a tiny difference in your mindset or maybe even a big difference? Would you like to do it again and maybe even incorporate this into a daily or weekly routine? Did you get inspired to add something else like a gentle turn of your head? Reflect on what you are feeling and maybe even try it again in another day or two and write about how you might feel different on different days.

Meditation Message 2: Eat mindfully and with presence and contentment.

Why: When I was in Yoga teacher training, they taught us about Ayurveda the ancient form of healing mainly through food and mindful eating. Some monks eat in complete silence and total devotion to the food in front of them. In reading *The Dalai Lama's Cat* by David Michie recently it all came back to me. Little Snow Lion (the cat) explains in the book in exquisite detail how something tastes, and reminds the reader that eating when totally present will enhance the flavor and the experience.

When I eat with total attention, and believe me it's a challenge for my monkey brain sometimes, the sense of satisfaction I get from eating drastically increases. My favorite thing to do is to close my eyes when I eat. Cutting out visual perception causes my taste receptors to come alive and the flavor seems to increase. I can really enjoy the different textures of the food in my mouth and how lovely it is to chew everything carefully. Digestion begins in your mouth, so chewing your food completely will help your tummy work less. It will also slow down your rate of food intake, thus allowing your brain to catch up with your stomach, and let you know when you are full before you are over-stuffed.

Your turn: Be completely present with your food for just one meal. You may even want to close your eyes while chewing your food and notice how the flavors change when you take your eyes out of the sensation equation. Write how you feel and what you noticed. You just might want to do it again and again!

Meditation Message 3: Everything is possible because perfection does not exist.

Why: What is perfection? Really, what is it? Is it what you think is perfect, or what I think is perfect? Because I can pretty much guarantee you right now your sense of perfection will be different than mine. The best advice I can give when being worried about being perfect is to just be you! Be the best you can be, and that will be wonderfully awesome! You already have your very best within you! I believe we all have a spark of God (or whatever you want to call the creator of all things) within us and he/she gave us free will to be whatever we want to be. We are wonderful just the way we are right now; and we have the power to be even better, we just have to choose to be better. But not perfect, because perfect is that spark within you. You already have it. You can stop worrying that you will never be perfect, you already have that spark within you; you just have to let it out.

Your turn: Write about your perception of perfection. Has it fooled you lately or maybe all of your life? Maybe your mother or other influential person in your life has told you what should be perfect. Can you realize that belief in perfection could be false and let go of your belief of a certain perfection perception you have been holding on to? How can you change your way of being hard on yourself (we are all our worst critic) by letting go of perfection?

Meditation Message 4: Everything is connected. The water coming from your faucet is the same water the dinosaurs peed in a long time ago.

Why: Well, that is called the hydrologic cycle, Google it, if you wish. But think about it. Trees are turned into paper, building materials, fuel to heat your home, etc. Water is not just water. It is contained in clouds, in lakes and rivers, in underground caves, etc. You drink and wash with the water coming from your faucet. It has been collected and cleaned up for you to use from rivers, lakes, or underground. You brush your teeth, make coffee or tea with that water. That water then returns into the cycle by you peeing it out, or simply flowing back into your sink, as you accidentally leave the faucet running too long and your cup overflows. Our bodies are also made of mostly water. Amazing, isn't it? And when we die, it begins again; that beautiful cycle of life, as we are returned to the Earth.

Your turn: Reflect on the seemingly fleeting moments that actually happen again and again. How trees grow leaves, drop them, and grow them again in the next season. Think about your daily activities and how things come and go. Reflect upon this magical cycle of life and how you are an active participant in that cycle.

Meditation Message 5: Be with yourself. Just for one minute. You might learn something amazing.

Why: During the course of each day, we have to be different people. The responsible adult who gets out of bed to go to work on time. The mother or father who coaxes their kid out of bed. We have to make choices to eat the proper food or feel terrible when we eat junk. We have to do a lot of things each day we may not necessarily want to do, but we do them because we know we have to or because it's the right thing to do. And I'm a Gemini! I have several faces! I usually come across as happy and confident. A coworker referred to me as bubbly. Yes, I'm a nice person. I love helping people and will always try to find empathy for everyone, even if they make me madder than hell. And I will easily slip into the mode of looking out for everyone else first. When I then drop exhausted on the couch one evening wondering why I am so terribly grumpy and tired, it hits me. I haven't really been myself in a while. And usually that is where it stays for another few days, because, hey, it's always easier to procrastinate on things that concern yourself. But then, after a few days, my tiredness will get the best of me, and it's time to just be. I close my eyes, maybe play some nice music, and I just AM. I am just being myself breathing, just being myself feeling the exhaustion and frustration of the past days when I was different versions of myself, but not truly myself. And I just am. And when I just am, amazing things happen. I realize that I actually wasn't serving my friends and family by putting them first. I realize when I snapped at a person I love so very much it wasn't because they were being stupid, it was because I was not being myself, and I got impatient. And then the five minutes glide away, but I feel refreshed and rejuvenated, because just for a few minutes, I was myself again. I was able to have a hissy fit inside and say what I wanted to say and now I feel better again. That, my friends, is the best form of mediation I have found so far.

Your turn: Reflect on how often in a day you do things that your true inner self would not want to do. While some of those things are necessary (like going to work to keep a steady income and a roof over your head), many of the things we do daily are really not necessary and not serving anyone, even though our ego tells us we *have* to do this for someone. Write about your feelings when you actually just sit and be yourself. Don't be shy to write out the nasties and the frustrations you may be feeling. Writing them on paper makes them leave your body, and that is a good thing. Release. Let go. Be yourself. Enjoy!

2. NAIKAN – THE ART OF GRATITUDE

My Reiki Teacher Bridget Lambert recommended the book *Naikan: Gratitude, Grace, and the Japanese Art of Self-Reflection* by Gregg Krech to me in one of our sessions. This book has changed my life. It taught me to be grateful for everything. And I mean every little thing! When you sit down to eat, I may say a prayer thanking Spirit/God for the food I am about to eat. Naikan goes further. It asks me to be grateful for the food I eat, for the person who stocked the grocery store where I got my food, the cashier, the person who delivered the food to the grocery store, the person who serviced the truck used to deliver that food to my grocery store, the farmer who planted the seeds that grew into the food in front of me, the seed for growing, the soil for allowing the seed to grow, the sun, air, and soil for providing the nutrition the seed needed to grow, and so on.

Naikan and practicing gratitude will teach you to slow down and enjoy the little things, as each and every little thing is part of a big thing. And that big thing is called the Universe.

Naikan Message 1: Practicing Gratitude in your daily life may cause an improvement in your attitude toward your surroundings.

Why: Naikan changed the way I thought about things and proved to me we are all one. Once you think about each activity in your life this way, you will most likely feel immensely humbled that you even exist. It is so easy to forget the little steps that are necessary to make anything happen.

There is a beautiful quote in the Naikan book, which really affected me. It is on page 47 of that powerful book:

"In the Midst of Pain

Once, not long ago, it was a hearty tree providing shade, food, and oxygen – a world of its own.

For a hundred years, perhaps more, it flourished with breath and life.

Then it was cut, sawed, ground, and pressed until it found itself softly resting between two friends.

Peacefully and patiently it waited for the moment it would burst forth into the world and exercise the meaning of its life.

And now that moment has come. It gracefully caressed my cheek, wiping the tears from my eyes and taking on my pain as its own.

All those years as seed, tree, wood, and tissue in preparation for the fleeting moment it would console my sadness.

As it gives its life to comfort me I almost failed to see the kindness of its deed.

Wrapped up in self-centered pain, tear-blinded, I nearly missed its selfless service. Who will give witness to such compassion if not me?

Shriveled and soaked, it died while serving a fool who discarded thousands of its brothers and sisters without a thanks — not one tear shed in gratitude.

Teach me to see through the teardrop, that in the midst of pain I may understand the true source of the softness against my face.

Teach me to cry with my eyes wide open."

Your turn: Write about a simple process that happens daily like getting the mail, eating, driving to work, turning on the light in the evening, etc. Think about ALL the things that have to happen (you may not even know them all, but really try to think about all the steps in the process) before that piece of mail arrives in your mail box or that piece of food in your mouth. Enjoy the experience of finding full awareness!

Naikan Message 2: Compassion helps you better deal with crazy people. You must remember that you can only control your own actions and reactions, so control your dissatisfied feelings (anger, frustration, etc.) by learning more compassion when someone upsets you.

Why: We don't/can't really know every detail of someone else's life to understand why/how they react to certain situations. The next time you don't like the way someone acts, try to respond with compassion. Just send the person a bubble of compassion and love. Make it your favorite color, or green, for healing, or pink, for love. Do not give away your power by getting aggravated or playing the victim. Two specific people in my life come to mind. They tried their best to be catty, snarky, rude, hurtful, and condescending. I realized these two people were so miserable in their lives, they had to try to put me down to feel better about themselves. This lifted a huge veil of sorrow off me, as I realized it really wasn't about me. The sorrow left me and true compassion entered into my heart for those two people. I felt truly sad for them. They must really be suffering to be that hurtful to others.

Your turn: Has someone hurt you? Can you imagine how they may be feeling? Going outside your place of hurt or being annoyed with that person, can you see why they may do the things they do? You may never know how they really feel, as we are never intimately part of their life's experiences, and we can never know how people react to certain challenges. Can you imagine how or why they are so difficult?

Naikan Message 3: Painful events suck, but they make us better people in the end.

Why: I've had my share of painful experiences from my childhood into adulthood. A little while ago my first-born kitty passed away after honoring me with her sassy body and Spirit for 16 years. As much as I'm hurting inside and missing her, I wouldn't give up all the memories she helped me make – even when she puked on my new carpet – I bought a little pet carpet cleaner robot thing. One of the coolest gadgets, if you ask me. There is something positive to be gleaned out of each event, even if you do not immediately see it.

Your Turn: What painful events are you grateful for now? Process and feel how far you have come. You can do this; you already have done so much! Everyone's journey is unique and marvelous. Even if you are in the midst of a painful event now, I can pretty much guarantee you that you are further along today than you were yesterday. So reflect on how far you have come. Own your greatness!

Naikan Message 4: When you feel yourself going to a place of judgment, stop, and send compassion.

Why: I caught myself judging a young woman recently. What I noticed is that I don't like judging anymore. I've been through too much in my life to now sit on my high horse pretending to know better than anyone else. I have been hurt by judgmental people in my life. So why would I do the thing I hate so much? To make myself feel better? Really? Does that really make me feel better? Nope! Compassion wins the day yet again! And I feel so much better now!

Your turn: Did you judge someone in the last day or week? Why? Write down how you can show compassion instead of judgment.

Naikan Message 5: Perspective is everything.

Why: When you are feeling grumpy because it's raining outside, think about how happy the plants are to get a thirst-quenching drink and for impurities in the air to be cleaned out instead. Sometimes our perspective is what makes us feel bad, not the situation. I often get caught up in my head and worry too much about little things that don't really matter in the grand scheme of things. I might judge myself if there is a speck of dirt on my floor. Some days I feel like a failure if my house isn't perfectly clean. The shift in perspective might come when I realize the reason why I skipped vacuuming this weekend was because I was having so much fun with my friends all day that I ran out of time. I can vacuum later. Friends are more important.

Your turn: Reflect on how changing your perspective about something you don't like doing might improve your feelings toward it. You may be able to gain perspective on why you dislike something or at least look at the situation from a different angle, which may allow you to feel better about it.

3. REIKI – THE UNIVERSAL ENERGY OF LOVE

I became a Reiki Master in 2016 and it has been my most powerful achievement so far. Reiki is a Japanese relaxation technique and a powerful healing tool. With all the Yoga and Shaman training I have had over the years, once I started learning about Reiki everything else clicked into place for me.

What is Reiki? It is a form of energy healing used to explain the spark of love energy we all have in our selves that connects us to each other and the Universe. It is the Universal energy that goes back to the source/God. By tapping into this powerful energy, one can release energy blocks, heal wounds in the past, and even project loving energy into the future.

Reiki can be hard to understand, but once you experience it, the feeling of deeply letting go and relaxing into your own beautiful energy and heart space, you will understand what the Universal power, Reiki/Love, really is.

Reiki has enabled me to let go of much of my anxiety (although, trust me, I still get anxious), and has allowed me to step into my heart to let my intuition to speak loudly and clearly. Reiki made me realize that whenever I follow my intuition, the result will be the best possible.

Since this is the Universal Energy of Love/Source, it knows best what the person receiving Reiki needs. So when my client tells me their knee is hurting, I would be inclined to put my hands on their knee and send healing energy. However, Reiki will know the reason why this knee is hurting. It might be hurting because there is some old trauma from a past-life stuck in the person's hips, causing a misalignment, thus causing knee pain. So Reiki will guide the energy into the hips instead of the knee, in this example. While this could be irritating (to not really know where to send the energy), it is also liberating, as it allows me to let go of any expectations and send Reiki to the person with the intention of helping for the highest good. This has really allowed me to let go of a lot of crap and has allowed me to simply become a clean vessel for Reiki to share with others, and often times, cause immediate relief from physical pain and improved mental well-being.

Reiki Message 1: Reiki – The Universal Energy of Love – Works!

Why: I have so many examples from my practice, but one that I love is my friend's dog was ill. I sent him Reiki and while he said he was ready to leave his body, he needed to stay to ensure my friend (his human) was okay. I was so worried and could tell my worry was getting in the way. So I sent another round of Reiki and asked for the outcome to be for the highest good of all involved. Less than 24 hours later, my friend calls to tell me she's been to the vet, got the dog new medication and the blood work results she was so worried about indicated the dog was in great shape for his age. Further, the treatment was half as much as she expected, and an old friend of hers, who she hadn't talked to in over 6 years, offered to pay for the dog's vet bills! Can you say amazing? I can't make this up! When you release your fears, and allow the Universe to help deliver the best-possible outcome, greater things than you can even imagine will happen!

Your turn: Even if you're not a Reiki practitioner, you can write down what you would like and then ask Spirit, Angels, whoever you feel comfortable asking, for the best possible outcome for you or the situation you are describing. Try to ask as open-minded as possible. Meaning, if you are asking for a new car, ask for a lovely reliable car that will get you where you need to go. Be sure to release this wish into the Universe once you are finished. Try not to continue describing or refining after you have sent that wish out to the Universe. Be open to what happens! It might happen immediately, tomorrow, the next week, or whenever the timing is right.

Reiki Message 2: Energy and Spirit is real.

Why: Have you noticed at some point in your life that certain people make you feel better when you see them or walk nearby? Some people seem to light up the room, while others seem to make your mood drop. Energy is real. When I welcome Reiki clients into my home, they immediately begin to relax. I have made my home a haven and the Reiki room has been surrounded by sacred Reiki symbols, which prepare the energy around us for clearing away the nasty stuff, and letting the good energy enter. Even if you don't believe in this, which is totally okay, you must have noticed that some people make you feel better than others.

Your turn: Write about who makes you feel good and who does not. Reflect on what it is about them that makes you feel a certain way. If you have no idea, no worries! Those people who make you feel bad, can you gently release them and not see them again? Or can you at least limit your exposure to those people who create trouble in your life?

Reiki Message 3: Love is Everything.

Why: All troubles can be solved or at least diminished by love. What is love? Love is care, compassion, empathy, and courage. You must be courageous to love the people who upset you.

Think about the people who make you mad. When I did this, I realized most are really miserable, and thus, are mean to you, to lift their misery – or at least they think it will make them feel better – and maybe it does temporarily. Look at them with pink glasses of love, as my Uncle used to say. You may also realize you see something in the person you are mad at that you don't like about yourself. Those have been the most challenging realizations for me. And that is when you need the most love sent; love to the other person and love to yourself.

Your turn: Identify the people who need more empathy in your life. Send them love and then consciously close the door of attachment to them. I do this by folding my hands in front of my chest in prayer pose and bowing my head to close the flow of energy between my heart and that person. Write down how you feel after closing the energetic door.

Reiki Message 4: Stop to smell the flowers.

Why: It's not just a hippie saying! When I actually really stop, bend down, and smell flowers in the parking lot or on a nature hike, it transforms me to the happy times in my childhood when I was sitting in the grass watching the bees fly around. Try it, you will not be disappointed. Just remember to bend at your knees so you don't hurt your back. And if you did not grow up with any nature around you that is perfectly okay. There is no time like now to stop and smell the flowers!

When you enjoy more of the little things in life you see how the universal energy of love moves through everything around you. The plants, animals, and humans are all affected by that love energy in some way.

Your turn: Write about what you noticed/felt when you smelled the flowers.

Reiki Message 5: Letting go and trusting makes magic happen.

Why: When you read books on Spirituality and praying, they tell you to say a prayer and then release it to God, trusting it will become true. But I have learned to take this a step further with Reiki. Reiki will only make the highest good happen. And Reiki will send the energy where it is really needed, as discussed before. At first, this drove me crazy. When my friend's head hurts, I want to place my hands on her head, and make it feel better. But Reiki may know that the headache stems from an old shoulder injury and will send the healing to that spot, thus alleviating the headache pain. I have had numerous experiences in my Reiki practice that show me this is so very true and so very important. Let go, send love, that is the best you can do for all involved. For example, a friend of mine texted me she was having a panic attack. I sent her Reiki and asked for healing to occur for the highest good. She calmed down almost immediately and then shared with me the next day the craziest thing happened, her pancreatitis is also not hurting anymore, when she has been in pain for nearly two years! Wow! I had no idea she was having additional health issues, but Reiki knew, and Reiki sent the healing where it needed to go. I could not have dreamed for all that healing to occur in one session. My limited understanding of the whole situation would have set me back in just fixing her panic attack.

Your turn: Practice letting go. When something bothers you, imagine it placed into a bubble of white light and send it to the Universe to be cleansed, never to return. You may also want to write down what is bothering you, then saying a sentence of blessing and consciously letting go, and then burning that sheet of paper (please be careful not to burn the house or the woods down in the process). You may want to place the sheet of paper into your kitchen sink or into your backyard barbeque grill and release all that funk into the Universe, never to return. See how wonderful it feels to really let go and open to receive the good coming at you.

4. SPIRITUALITY – WHAT IT MEANS TO YOU

Spirituality to me is not a religion or any particular Spiritual path. Some people are religious; they will go to church every Sunday because they feel they have to, but the rest of the week, they will not really think about it much, but they believe they are doing what they should be doing to be a good person. A Spiritual person will seek to find the Spark/God (or whatever you want to call this marvelous being), that Spark that is within all of us. I truly believe that everyone is Spiritual. We begin as children with the ability to see what many adults cannot anymore (which is a complete tragedy, and I hope to help you find this Spark again). I have had several friends with children who told me their kid has an imaginary friend and roll their eyes. But my reaction was always instinctively to nod encouragingly and smile. I did not realize why I did that until a few years ago, when I realized we all have at least one imaginary friend or Spirit guide, but may have forgotten about it, as we grew up. I think Spirituality has a lot to do with letting go and being silent with yourself. Being present. Noticing the small things that seem obvious, but are so very exceptional, once you give it a moment to think about.

Consider the monarch butterfly. This magnificent creature is not only stunningly beautiful, it has an amazingly long migration route from Mexico to the United States and back. But wait, there's more! The migration is so long, not a single butterfly's lifespan is long enough, so this migration is done over several generations. What, you say? Heidi has gone mad. Nope, look it up! It's incredible! The National Wildlife Federation website explains how most monarch butterflies do not live more than a few weeks. There are about three to five generations born each spring and summer and most of the offspring do not live beyond five weeks. The exception is the last generation born at the end of the summer. This last generation of each year is the over-wintering generation that must make the journey back to Mexico. Rather than breeding immediately, the over-wintering monarchs fly back to Mexico and stay there until the following spring. In the early spring, they fly north to the southern United States and breed. Over-wintering monarch butterflies can live over eight months.

My mother used to own a home in Pacific Grove, California, otherwise known as Butterfly Town, USA. This northern California small town would welcome the butterflies during migration season. I was completely blown away when I visited one year as an adult, and watched these beautiful creatures cluster in the hundreds in a grove of large trees. The most magical and Spiritual thing to me was you could not hear them – there was no sound! These little creatures fly practically silent! Watching Nature's miracle to me is Spiritual. So where am I going with this? Many magical places, stick with me! Think about this. How does a monarch butterfly know when he or she is supposed to over-winter or just live for a few weeks? How does the butterfly know where to go? His mother didn't get to teach him like other migratory animals who show their offspring where to go during migration. How is this possible? I would argue it's that Spark, that Spirit we all have in ourselves. Does this make any sense to you? Does it at least intrigue you to think about it some more? I hope it does. Thinking about the magic that surrounds us in Nature makes me a more Spiritual person, and I hope to kindle that curiosity in you to investigate what makes you interested in the magic of this Universe and finding your Spirituality.

How can a being, no matter its size (even though a tiny butterfly is even more amazing in my eyes) know what to do without someone telling it? I believe that is Spirituality, it is that Spark we all have. It is the magic that is life on this Planet. And the mystery of it all, and not driving yourself crazy to try to understand, that is true Spirituality to me. The wonder of it all makes it Spiritual and magical. Let's explore our Spirituality now. Let's play and be wowed by the amazing life we have, even if we have bad days.

Spirituality Message 1: Silence is Magical

Why: In the silence is where all things lie. When I get a quiet moment in the day, it seems as if everything shifts in to the Spiritual/Magical gear, and I notice things I had not noticed all day until then. I like to reflect on how I can improve the silence. Most of the time silence is so beautiful I will be content with the silence and not want to change anything.

Your turn: Be silent for just a few minutes and notice how it shifts your awareness. You may have a moment of impatience, wondering when this moment of silence is over, or thinking about your to-do list. It is okay and part of the process of beginning to be happier in your daily life by noticing the little things. You may also hear nothing but street noise outside; feel free to put in some ear plugs and notice how that shifts your awareness. Write about how you felt the first time you sat quietly. Hopefully you'll be intrigued enough to continue practicing this daily, even just for a few minutes. Write about how each time may be different or the same.

Spirituality Message 2: We are all One

Why: Because we are. Trust me. Seriously though, have you felt déjà vu, that feeling that this moment has happened already? This can be attributed to the fact that we are all connected and have at some point in the life of the Universe experienced what you are currently experiencing. A friend of mine had a discussion with Spirit, and I was honored when she shared what she learned. She wanted to know why some people are convinced, for example, that they were a Roman soldier in a past life, and another person may have the same memory. The way it was described to my friend by Spirit, is that we are part of a big bucket of memories. All one, and all part of this Being that some of us call God. Each time one of us, our Soul, decides to come back to Earth to fulfill a challenge or life lesson we want to achieve, we take information from that bucket and that is how we all get similar memories. Because we are all one. Isn't that a fascinating thought? Whether it is true or not makes no difference to me. My intuition tells me it is true, but maybe it does not resonate with you, and that is okay. What I want to get across is that we are all connected. Surely, you have had a thought about a friend and a few minutes or seconds later that friend has phoned or texted. It is because we are all connected, my dear!

Your turn: Contemplate on this thought. We are all one. Does it scare you or make you happy? Think of a person you love dearly. You most likely have no problem thinking about being One with this person. What about a person who you dislike? How can you be One with this person? Can you write out why you don't like this person? Maybe it's something you don't like about yourself? Maybe you don't know, but can you imagine and write about how you could be One even with a person you don't like? Good luck, this is a big challenging subject! Be gentle with yourself! Just thinking about this will open your mind to greater possibilities of happiness.

Spirituality Message 3: Spirituality is real! Just open your heart and listen!

Why: The truth about Spirituality is revealed to you by opening your heart and being quiet enough to hear what it says. When I quiet my mind and heart, often by counting to 4 slowly while inhaling and then counting to 4 slowly while exhaling as previously mentioned, my heart/intuition begins to speak and I slow down and notice the little things my mind just flew over. The little chirp of the bird outside saying hello, the blood flowing in my veins, my cat's peaceful breathing while he sleeps. And I notice other things, too. I notice my higher-self whispering to me loving things like I'm worth it, I deserve happiness, or I am a wonderful and compassionate person, and I deserve to be at peace. Sometimes I even sense in my mind's ear the message from God/Spirit/Angels and I can feel how much I am truly loved and supported, even when my brain does not feel it all the time.

Your turn: Have you experienced Magic or something you really can't explain and can only call Spiritual? Have you heard or sensed messages in your mind's ear that were without a doubt audible to you in some way? If you feel that you have not yet experienced this, reflect on how you would like to experience the magic of Spirituality. Go ahead, put in that order now, so you can begin to feel connected with the One Source, so you can begin to feel Spirituality, as we all deserve to feel it.

Spirituality Message 4: Staying present can lead to Spirituality.

Why: Your mind is very powerful and can either make you feel wonderful or very bad. Anxiety in my life has made it difficult for me to do things sometimes. My anxiety is especially high when I am not present. I worry about things that haven't even happened yet, or fret over things that happened yesterday or a year ago, or even longer. When I have a good day and I can stay present, I live life to its fullest! I enjoy the air I breathe, I enjoy the food I eat to its fullest (sight, sound, smell, taste, consistency or texture on my tongue, etc.), and I remain in the moment for as long as I can...until the next moment comes. And then I stay in that moment until the following moment!

Some people talk about meditation being a great way to stay present, and with that comes finding yourself and finding your Spirit self, your Soul. This Soul prefers very much to be present and to be happy in the moment, even if the moment may not be favorable toward you. The next moment will come, trust me, and it will be better! Trust your Spirit, trust your Soul, and remain Present. I feel much closer to God, Spirit, our eternal source when I am present. And in that sweet spot is when I feel the most Spiritual. I hope you practice with me, so we can stay in the sweet spot longer...maybe one day we will stay there all the time.

Your turn: Reflect on how being present can lead to your Spirituality. Can being present get you over a hump you have felt like you will not be able to conquer? Will being present show you the way out? Write about how you feel when you practice being present.

Spirituality Message 5: Spirituality and belief in the higher good is essential to happiness.

Why: I get disillusioned when I watch the nightly news on television. It causes me anxiety and I feel depressed thinking all this drama is happening and I can't do anything about it. We can debate about ratings and getting the story for those ratings, but all I'll say about it is that I have noticed when there is a particularly large house fire in a city (for example), all of a sudden there are more reports on house fires on the news for the coming few days...until something else happens that can be exploited. Have you noticed that? Either way, maybe you love watching the news, and that is perfectly fine. But it makes me sad, anxious, and depressed, so I have chosen to stay out of the mainstream media mayhem. I recently listened to the Doreen Virtue Angel Summit online and she had a speaker stating he doesn't watch the news anymore because that vibration doesn't serve. This really resonated with me. We can choose to add a joyful, happy vibration to the Planet's energy, or a fearful one. I choose Happiness.

Your turn: Reflect on events and how they make you feel. Can you make them better in your mind or improve on the Spiritual vibration that you are contributing to the Planet? How does raising your vibration get you closer to Spirituality? Enjoy exploring your beliefs, fears, and hopes.

5. HEALING TOOLS – CONTINUE FINDING HAPPINESS

This section is intended for you to get ideas on what can help you to continue to feel better and heal some old wounds you may be carrying with you. Healing is making whole. Some authors and especially Shamans will remind you that no matter what disease you have, you can still die from it, but you can heal your Soul before you pass into the next stage of life or death.

Holding on to old trauma serves no one and hurts you the most. Let's practice letting go together. I have let go of a lot in my lifetime already, and there is still plenty opportunity to continue healing and making good memories. Tools that have helped me include antidepressants, therapy, and the tools listed below. I hope you find these tools helpful, as you can implement them anywhere and anytime you need to heal and let go.

Healing Tools Message 1: Music can heal you.

Why: Music evokes emotions in the listener – helps process feelings, relieve stress, and invoke happy memories. I will always remember where I was the time I heard certain songs: the first slow love song I danced with my first boyfriend. Moving close to his body; the exhilaration I felt for being so close to him and the sense of doing something new. The song my favorite Zumba teacher played on my birthday in class that made my whole body happy. Make memories last longer by listening to music. Happy memories, preferably.

Your turn: Listen to an uplifting, fast song and then listen to a slow song. How did those two songs make you feel? Reflect on how music can affect your mood and choose to listen to music that makes you happy more often.

Healing Tools Message 2: Read books that inspire you.

Why: Some of my favorite books include *Happier at Home* by Gretchen Ruben, *The Suburban Safari* by Hannah Holmes, *A Sand County Almanac* by Aldo Leopold, anything by Paulo Coelho (especially *Veronica Decides to Die*), and Angel books by Doreen Virtue. Going outside yourself brings you back to yourself. When we remain in our head for too long, we get disconnected with Nature, people, reality, and we may feel very unbalanced and empty. Peace returns when you can return to yourself.

Your turn: Are there books you have been meaning to read for a while? Read, even just 5 minutes daily, and I can pretty much guarantee you will feel more connected to yourself. If you don't have a list, I encourage you to either browse your favorite online book store, or even better, go to your local book store and look at the books available in a section that inspires you. It doesn't have to be the self-help section. Many fiction books, especially books from Paulo Coelho, are considered fiction, but have many real-life elements in them, so you can still learn something from them.

Healing Tools Message 3: There is a Yoga practice for everyone.

Why: I started learning about Yoga in community college. Hatha/Iyengar Yoga's focus is on alignment and strength. A few years later I was not sure I wanted to stay in my field of floodplain management. So I enrolled in the 200-hour Yoga Teacher Training program. It was a strenuous 9-month journey. I learned each stage of life is supposed to have a different Yoga practice – not at all like Western Yoga! Strenuous, hot Yoga with a lot of movement is supposed to be done when you're young, then more calming, soothing Yoga, and then mostly meditation in your older years of life.

So if you feel your practice, if you have one, is missing something or makes you feel out of balance, it's probably time to adjust the form of Yoga you practice. You do Yoga everyday by just being the best you can be and being nice to people. See, you're a Yogi and didn't even know it! You don't have to make yourself into a pretzel to be a Yogi.

Viniyoga has been my go-to for years. It combines breath and gentle movement, and is therapeutic for anxiety, depression, back pain; you name it.

After Yoga, you should feel calmer, more balanced, and centered, rejuvenated, and energized, but not too hot. Many Westerners practice Yoga for exercise and to build their ego rather than their muscles. That is not what true Yoga is about.

Your turn: Do you practice Yoga? If you have a favorite pose, what do you love about it? If you do not practice Yoga, imagine what could make you feel better today. Could you just stretch your arms over head and breathe deeply? Sure, that's Yoga! Could you stand comfortably, and then bend forward to stretch your back and give your body a slight inversion? That's Yoga! Could you just sit and breathe for 5 minutes? That is Yoga as well, it's called Pranayama! Reflect on the type of Yoga or movement your body and soul would benefit from the most at this time. Keep in mind it might change later, so feel free to keep adding to your journal!

Healing Tools Message 4: Make time to play every day – even for 5 minutes.

Why: Play lightens our hearts and lets our creativity come out. Play helps me relax and just be me for a little bit. I try not to beat myself up if I don't know how to play that day. Maybe I just listen to my favorite song for a few minutes if I'm not feeling all that creative that day. And sometimes listening to the song will cause me to get more energy and do something more than just listen. Maybe I stand up and dance. That is one of my favorite activities. I really feel that dance is a healing tool and goes with music (obviously) to help you feel better. Songs, however, can alter your mood, so be sure to pick a happy song. Other ways to play include writing in a journal, doodle or draw, skip instead of walking to the mail box, swing at the playground, or even just lying on the floor to read instead of sitting on a chair. Kick your feet up and read on your stomach a little while. See how that makes you feel.

Your turn: Remember, you can! What can you do today to lighten your mood and play more? Would creating a list so you can fall back on that during the days you're not feeling creative help? Reflect on little things you can do to increase your happiness. Text a friend, watch the birds outside, pet your cat or dog, what else would make you happy?

Healing Tools Message 5: There is no one way to feel better.

Why: People may tell you, try this, not that, if you want to feel better. But that one thing may have helped that person, and only them. You are a beautiful unique spark among the Universe! Although we are all connected, and certain things may make several of us feel better, it will certainly not make everyone better. Our uniqueness and our connectedness, however, can support our Journey through life, as you can learn from others what helped them, and try it yourself. I believe that is why you are reading this journal, and I am eternally grateful that you are! I also want you to know that because something may have made you feel better in the past doesn't mean it will always make you feel better. Part of our life's journey is to remember to try new things. Being in a rut never makes me feel good, even if it takes me courage to get out of that rut, in the end it's worth it.

Your turn: Reflect on a belief you may have that you feel cannot/should not be changed. This may be challenging, but I know you can do it! Is there a belief you have you think everyone should have? For example, if you are a cat person, you may think everyone should have a cat (I would agree with you, since I love cats, but not everyone is fit to be a good cat person, and some people may be allergic!). Reflect on why you feel so strongly and see how you can open your mind to be more gentle about that belief. Flexibility and gentleness will serve your body and mind and increase happiness.

CONCLUSION

I sincerely appreciate you taking the time to read the messages in this book, sit with them, and reflect on them in your own way.

You may wish to re-read or re-write some of your thoughts after a while. This would be very beneficial, as we are all different each day, and can learn something new about us daily. Continue to enjoy the journey!

I hope I was able to contribute to your happiness in a small way and show you there are many tools to help you feel better, even when you think there is no hope.

I trust you are able to glean what you need from this journal and continue your journey to happiness.

We all have that divine spark within us. We all have the potential for greatness. Let's ignite that spark together and fly! Spread your wings my dear, you deserve to be happy!

IN GRATITUDE

T hank you to my husband who supports me, no matter what crazy project I want to try next. Thank you for your ever-calming presence in my life.

Thank you, Tracee for supporting me, coaching me through the writing process and taking the time to get an outline figured out.

Thank you, Heather for being my Spirit guide and always being there for me when I need a helping hand, a salad to eat, a laugh, or a hug.

Thank you, Samantha for helping me brain storm and being so supportive and allowing me to bounce ideas off you.

Thank you to all my teachers who have supported me in my journey. It would have been much more difficult without your love and encouragement.

Thank you to everyone I love. You know who you are!

ABOUT THE AUTHOR

happiness

Heidi Carlin is the owner of Reiki with Heidi, LLC. She is a Registered Yoga Teacher, Reiki Master, and Essential Oil Enthusiast, among many things.

In her journey to deal with depression and anxiety, she collected the many tools described in this journal book to be happier and deal with anxiety and depression on a daily basis.

This collection of tools are all self-help related and can be done by anyone who is ready to start walking on the road to happiness.

Heidi lives in Austin, Texas, USA with her husband and cat. She enjoys reading, hiking, traveling, and cooking.

Printed in the United States
By Bookmasters